PAST PRESENT

ASTORIA

OPPOSITE: Taken from the hilltop behind the Flavel house (in the lower center of the frame), this c. 1890 image reveals Astoria's close connection to the Columbia River. Physically built atop pilings set into the river, water peeks through any undeveloped areas of the city's downtown. (Courtesy of Clatsop County Historical Society [CCHS] Sovey Collection No. 52.001.100.)

ASTORIA

Dr. Chelsea K. Vaughn of the
Clatsop County Historical Society

To Amaru, the silliest bit of sunshine in my day, and to R of the unforgettable integrity

Copyright © 2023 by Dr. Chelsea K. Vaughn of the Clatsop County Historical Society

ISBN 978-1-4671-0958-1

Library of Congress Control Number: 2022949299

Published by Arcadia Publishing
Charleston, South Carolina

Printed in the United States of America

For all general information, please contact Arcadia Publishing:
Telephone 843-853-2070
Fax 843-853-0044
E-mail sales@arcadiapublishing.com
For customer service and orders:
Toll-Free 1-888-313-2665

Visit us on the Internet at www.arcadiapublishing.com

ON THE FRONT COVER: Looking west on Commercial Street from the corner of Tenth Street, these images juxtapose two different ideas of Astoria against a shared backdrop. The upper photograph, from the late 1940s, offers an ever-modernizing street scene with the city's historic architecture buried beneath a wall of neon signs. Still an active stretch of road, in the lower image, the neon has given way to a more subdued approach that better reflects the buildings' historical character. (Past image, courtesy of CCHS No. 6809-903.)

ON THE BACK COVER: Seen from the Columbia River, this turn-of-the-century waterfront view shows the saloons and hotels that once clustered at the base of Fourteenth Street. Behind them are St. Mary's Hospital (recognizable by the cross on its roof) and city hall (immediately to its left). Of all these buildings, only the city hall remains and now serves as the Heritage Museum. (Courtesy of CCHS No. 8930-906.)

CONTENTS

Acknowledgments   vii
Introduction   ix

1.   Coming to Town   11

2.   Staying the Night   27

3.   Commercial Street   43

4.   Around Town   65

5.   Long-Term Residents   83

ACKNOWLEDGMENTS

Thank you to everyone associated with the Clatsop County Historical Society, whose diligent efforts over the decades preserving Astoria's past have made my work significantly easier. All of the "past" photographs used in this book come from CCHS's permanent collection, housed in the Liisa Penner Research Center and Archives at the Heritage Museum. "Present" images are courtesy of the author.

For their particular help on this book, I would first like to thank Liisa Penner and John Goodenberger, whose immense knowledge of Astoria's history and its built environment successfully answered any question I might pose to them. Thank you to Haleigh Nagle for her work as a research assistant, both in identifying potentially interesting historical photographs and doing the research to justify their interest. Thank you to Michael Wentworth for his years of dedicated work digitizing the CCHS photograph collection. Thank you to Matt Powers for helping me to capture so many of the "Present" images, especially when that work involved donning fluorescent vests or climbing atop a van to get the proper shot. Thank you also to Finn Vaughn Hume for accompanying me on photo shoots, and photo-bombing my pictures every time I became too intent on taking "just one more photo to get it right." Thank you to Julie Burpee for looking over every bit of text I placed before you and constantly fixing my poor use of commas. Finally, thank you to Ryan Hume. You are my first and best reader, your ideas consistently move me forward, and my writing is better because of you.

INTRODUCTION

The Astoria of today has its origins in the devastating fire of December 8, 1922, that decimated the city's downtown, destroying nearly 300 businesses and displacing almost 2,000 people from their homes. Joined in mutual trauma, Astorians came together in a shared recovery. Before the fire was fully extinguished, people were already working to help one another, keeping each other apprised of new developments, providing food and clothing to those who had lost everything, and opening their homes to those in need of shelter. This same sense of urgency and collective purpose would continue as the city sought to rebuild. Much of the city's downtown was constructed in the years immediately following the fire. Many of these same buildings still stand today.

Economic decline and revitalization also played an important role in shaping the city. Marked by a history of booms and busts, the prosperity that Astoria enjoyed following World War II all but disappeared by the century's end as major industries moved elsewhere. Even in the early postwar years of relative comfort, Astoria's citizens felt the tensions between the pulls of modernity and preservation as early jewels of the city fell into disrepair. Two such examples from the late 1940s would be instructive in the years to come: the Flavel House mansion and the site of the original Fort Astoria. Seen as outdated remnants of other eras, both faced the threat of being turned into parking lots. Organizers working under the banner of the Clatsop County Historical Society and affiliated groups successfully saved both spaces, turning the house into a museum and the fort into a park.

Lessons learned from the Flavel House, Fort Astoria, and other early endeavors of the Historical Society and like-minded organizations created a template for navigating the city's often-rough transition from an economy based on natural resource extraction to one that depended upon outside interest in the area. With the logging and fishing industries largely diminished the need to attract others became evident. Astoria did not invent the idea of restoring its historic charms as a means of bringing new visitors to the city, but doing so fit well with Astorians' interest in preserving their past. Imagining a new Astoria meant embracing the old. Downtown buildings were returned to their original appearance, sites from the riverfront to the Astoria Column atop Coxcomb Hill were renewed, and many of the city's historic homes were restored.

This process also caught the attention of the film industry. With a well-preserved commercial district and historic homes situated on the banks of the Columbia River surrounded by a wooded hillside, Astoria became a popular location to make both movies and television shows. While the origins of Astoria-made cinema encompass the larger history of movies generally (the first movie filmed in Astoria, *The Fisherman's Bride* in 1909, is also the first known feature film made in Oregon), the prevalence of Astoria-made movies has steadily increased over the past few decades. Beginning with *The Goonies* in 1985, at least a dozen films have used the small town of Astoria as their backdrop.

The images that follow often capture this Astoria, the one of a revitalization marked by efforts to return historic buildings to their original appearance and to dot the city's landscape with parks and other natural spaces. The past scenes—whatever grittiness they may have originally held—are made picturesque by the passage of time and the filter of being caught in a stark black and white. At the same time, the present pictures tend to demonstrate restoration projects in their later stages. Absent from many of the past and present photographs are the in-between periods. Important still are the times when the historic structures' architectural details were buried beneath aluminum siding and oversized awnings, when Astoria was marked with empty storefronts and abandoned spaces, and when too many homes were succumbing to decay. This transitionary period allowed Astorians to clearly define their hopes and expectations for their small city. The Astoria of today stands as a testament to the town's appreciation of its history and its dedication to preserving this past.

CHAPTER

COMING TO TOWN

During the 1960s, this sign greeted visitors to Astoria as they entered from the east. Though known at the time more for its fishing than tourist industry, the sign still offered numerous sites that eager visitors might enjoy, many of which are still open today. (Courtesy of CCHS No. 30,438-400C.)

A dock at the base of Seventeenth Street has served Astoria travelers and commerce since at least the 1870s with the construction of the Farmer's Dock. By the 1880s, the Oregon Railway & Navigation Company (OR&N) had replaced this dock with one of their own. The current dock at Seventeenth Street hosts US Coast Guard vessels, the retired lightship the *Columbia*, and Columbia River cruise boats. (Past image, courtesy of CCHS No. 4425-340.)

S.S. ROSE CITY LEAVING O.R.&N.DOCK. ASTORIA.OR. 244.

Launched in 1888 by OR&N, the *T.J. Potter* transported passengers to and from Astoria until 1916. Noted for its luxury, the *Potter* was one of a few side-wheeled steamboats on the Columbia River. After being converted briefly to shipyard barracks, salvagers stripped the *Potter* in 1925 and left it on the north bank of Youngs Bay south of Astoria. The *Potter's* remains are still visible in this location during low tide. (Past image, courtesy of CCHS No. 22.015.017.)

Astorians flooded the city's train station ahead of Vice Pres. Charles Fairbanks visiting in 1907. Built to accommodate rail traffic with the opening of a train line to Portland in 1898, this all-wooden structure was replaced by a new brick station in 1925. Passenger service continued until 1952 and freight service until 1970. The once-abandoned building now serves as the Columbia River Maritime Museum's Barbey Maritime Center. (Past image, courtesy of CCHS Sovey Collection No. 052.001.017.)

Completed in 1896, the train trestle across the mouth of Youngs Bay connected Astoria via rail to the seaside resort towns southwest of the city. This line served a largely tourist market as vacationers from Portland and other areas east of Oregon's coastal range sought refuge from the summer heat in the cooler coastal climate. A car bridge opened in 1964 now follows this same route. (Past image, courtesy of CCHS No. 99.034.001.388.)

SEASIDE TRAIN CROSSING YOUNGS BAY, ASTORIA, OREG.
250.

A welcome arch across Commercial Street greeted visitors to Astoria's 1911 centennial celebration. While there were an increasing number of automobiles in Astoria, the vast majority of Centennial visitors arrived by train, with the railroad company offering special rates. Today, the retired pilot boat the *Peacock* offers visitors a glimpse of the town's maritime roots as they journey past the same point, now on Marine Drive. (Past image, courtesy of CCHS No. 99.034.001.)

COMING TO TOWN

Between 1910 and 1924, the Pacific Power and Light Company operated streetcars that served the neighborhoods of Uniontown to the west and Alderbrook to the east. While the streetcar lines are long gone, the Astoria Riverfront Trolley now utilizes the railroad tracks along the river's edge to facilitate a similar crosstown trek. The adjoining Riverwalk Trail allows foot and bicycle traffic along the city's scenic riverfront. (Past image, courtesy of CCHS No. 87.037.001.)

Clatsop Crest

Bradley State Scenic Viewpoint offers one of the few rest stops for travelers along Oregon Highway 30 between Astoria and Portland. Built upon land donated to the Oregon Highway Commission in 1921, the stop provided relief to the increasing auto tourism by providing a restroom, concession stand, and scenic views of the Columbia River below. While the concession stand is now gone, the scenic views remain. (Past image, courtesy of CCHS No. 12244-281.)

COMING TO TOWN

The covered bridge over the John Day River was built in 1918, as part of the new Columbia River Highway. Commissioned at the height of World War I, the bridge was constructed of wood as steel was in short supply. This bridge was replaced by a newer bridge in 1933, which, in turn, was replaced by the current bridge over the John Day River in the mid-1980s. (Past image, courtesy of CCHS No. 99.071.001.)

Entrance portals once flanked both sides of the Old Columbia River Highway near Fifty-Fourth Street in Alderbrook. Construction on the portals began in 1926, and they were officially dedicated in August 1927. By 1939, the highway had been realigned so that the majority of traffic into Astoria no longer drove past the portals. This portion of the old road became federal property during World War II. (Past image, courtesy of CCHS Ball Studio Collection No. 81.013.783.)

In the early 20th century, drivers entered Astoria from the east by following a series of roadways. Franklin Street cut over at Twenty-Third Street, bypassing the one-time primary roadway, Exchange Street, for Commercial Street. These became Marine Drive in the mid-1950s, a major thoroughfare that also combined portions of Astor, Bond, and Taylor Streets. Standard Oil in the earlier image and the hospital sign in the later mark the intersection of Twenty-Third and Exchange Streets. (Past image, courtesy of CCHS No. 6188-400S.)

Once known colloquially as "Park Road," Williamsport Road wraps along the southeastern edge of Astoria, connecting what was City (now Shively) Park to Youngs Bay below. Driving an early 1900s Orient Buckboard automobile, Henry Cyrus (pictured above) and photographer Elmer Coe continued their travels south, becoming the first to make the 30-mile trek between Astoria and Seaside by automobile. (Past image, courtesy of CCHS No. 1922-281.)

The bridge commonly referred to as the "Old Youngs Bay Bridge," spans the mouth of the Youngs River as it flows into Youngs Bay. Completed in 1921, the bridge connected Astoria to the Oregon Coast Highway. Though still in use, the completion of a larger bridge in 1964 and the rerouting of the highway have reduced the traffic on this bridge to mostly local travelers. (Past image, courtesy of CCHS No. 87.080.112.)

D. 55. HIGHWAY DRAWBRIDGE OVER YOONGS RIVER, ASTORIA, OREGON.

The so-called "new" Youngs Bay Bridge opened in 1964. Nearly one mile in length, the bridge connected Astoria at its southwestern point to the nearby town of Warrenton and greatly increased the traffic capacity along the newly rerouted Oregon Highway 101 to the Oregon Coast. The still-under-construction Astoria-Megler bridge that would connect Astoria to Washington State was visible to attendees of the New Youngs Bay Bridge dedication. (Past image, courtesy of CCHS No. 7809-282.)

Above, Oregon governor Mark Hatfield and his family depart the *M.R. Chessman* following its final voyage between Megler, Washington, and the Astoria Ferry Station at the foot of Fourteenth Street. The use of ferries in Astoria started by the 1840s. Regular service commenced in 1921 with the State of Oregon taking over transport in 1946. The 1966 completion of the Astoria-Megler Bridge officially ended ferry service to Astoria. (Past image, courtesy of CCHS No. 01.016.017.)

The four-mile-long bridge across the Columbia River from Astoria to Point Ellice, Washington was completed in August 1966, replacing a long-running ferry system. Often dismissed as the "Bridge to Nowhere," the Astoria-Megler Bridge exceeded expectations for the amount of traffic it would carry. As a result, the toll was removed on December 24, 1993—over two and a half years ahead of schedule. (Past image, courtesy of CCHS No. 87.089.016.)

COMING TO TOWN

STAYING THE NIGHT

Built following a devastating fire that destroyed much of Astoria's downtown on December 8, 1922, the luxurious Astoria Hotel demonstrated the city's ability to rebuild following the tragedy. With limited accommodations and thousands displaced by the fire, plans for the Astoria Hotel were expanded to include additional floors and guest rooms. (Courtesy of CCHS No. 008.056.007.)

The first hotel named Astoria stood at Seventeenth and Duane Streets. Opening in 1875 as O'Brian's, it was destroyed in the 1922 fire. City hall and Saint Mary's Hospital are visible behind the hotel to the right, while the Shively School bell tower is on the left. Of these buildings, only the city hall remains and now serves as the Clatsop County Historical Society's Heritage Museum, including the Liisa Penner Research Center and Archives. (Past image, courtesy of CCHS No. 04.024.003.)

The Astor House sat between Eleventh and Twelfth Streets on Duane Street. Originally built on pilings over a bay, the bay would be filled and the streets placed on solid ground. Still, in 2010, this site collapsed revealing the basement of a later building. The block has since been designated as Heritage Square and, besides the fenced-off basement, hosts the Garden of Surging Waves, the Astoria Sunday Market, and the American Legion building. (Past image, courtesy of CCHS No. 07.060.013.)

Among the older hotels in Astoria, the Occident Hotel met with controversy in 1899 when its all-White wait staff quit in protest of working for a Black supervisor, the hotel's longtime steward Benjamin Gayle. The Occident's owners backed Gayle and hired new waiters. The Occident continued as a hotel until its destruction in the 1922 fire. The new structure built in its place no longer hosted overnight guests, but still bears the Occident name. (Past image, courtesy of CCHS No. 3539-190.)

In the late 19th century, Travelers' Rest accommodated visitors to what would become the south side of Astoria on Youngs Bay, including workers for Craig Logging. Then called Williamsport, the one-time town name survives as that of a nearby roadway, though all that remains of Travelers' Rest are the original pilings on which it sat. (Past image, courtesy of CCHS No. 21.053.008.)

Opened in 1903, the Gold Star Hotel sat next to Astoria's train depot and featured a saloon, dining room, and lunch counter to accommodate those arriving by rail. To fit in the odd space between the depot and Commercial Street (now Marine Drive), the west or front end of the hotel was significantly narrower than its east or back side. (Past image, courtesy of CCHS No. 29022-400G.)

STAYING THE NIGHT

Another establishment catering to train travelers, the Depot Exchange—pictured above in 1910—sat across the intersection of Commercial (now Marine Drive) and Twentieth Streets from the Gold Star. Offering visitors a range of accommodations, including baggage delivery and autos for hire, the Depot Exchange operated until the late 1910s when it was converted to apartments before being torn down. The longtime site of the County Fairgrounds, it now houses the Astoria Aquatic Center. (Past image, courtesy of CCHS No. 20.024.092.)

Located on the northwest corner of Fourteenth and Commercial Streets, the Leyde Hotel was badly damaged in a 1914 fire, repaired, then destroyed in a 1916 fire. This second fire burned for over two hours and affected at least 16 other Commercial Street businesses, causing $60,000 in losses. A new building made of brick in the same location survived the great 1922 fire—though its interior was gutted. (Past image, courtesy of CCHS No. 19.009.003.)

The Hotel Tighe loomed over Exchange Street below. Becoming the Arlington Hotel by the 1910s, this building survived the 1922 Astoria fire and continued to provide lodging into the 1950s when it was torn down. The Tighe's lot now sits empty behind the one-time Telephone building turned law offices and a car dealership turned Astoria Senior Center. (Past image, courtesy of CCHS No. 3693-100.)

Advertisements for the Weinhard-Astoria Hotel (on the northeast corner of Twelfth and Duane Streets) touted a reinforced concrete basement, a pressurized brick superstructure, and terra cotta trimmings—features that would presumably make it fire-resistant. Yet, the building still succumbed during the December 8, 1922 fire. Its concrete exterior provided limited protection when the fire entered through the windows and ignited its wooden interior—effectively burning the building from the inside out. (Past image, courtesy of CCHS No. 14766-400W.)

STAYING THE NIGHT

Little remained of the Weinhard-Astoria Hotel following the Great Astoria Fire of 1922. Among the ruins, the hotel's entrance portal—which once greeted visitors on Duane Street—survived and would be relocated to City (later Shively) Park near Sixteenth and Williamsport Road. Placed over one of the park's many walking paths, the portal serves as an important connection to Astoria's past. (Past image, courtesy of CCHS No. 4264-935.)

The Page Building, on the southwest corner of Twelfth and Commercial Streets, served as the original location for both longtime business Owl Drugs and the first Merwyn Hotel. Destroyed in the devastating fire of December 8, 1922, Owl Drugs quickly reopened and would go on to occupy several storefronts at or near Twelfth and Commercial, including one built on the site of the Page Building. (Past image, courtesy of CCHS Sovey Collection No. 052.001.043.)

A second Merwyn Hotel opened three blocks from the original in 1925 on Duane Street between Tenth and Eleventh Streets. Originally serving travelers on short-term stays, the Merwyn eventually became a residential hotel in which people would rent rooms for an extended period of time, before being closed in 1989. The building subsequently sat empty and fell into disrepair until it was restored and opened as low-income housing in 2021. (Past image, courtesy of CCHS No. 22.001.068.)

Similar to the Merwyn, the once-popular Elliott Hotel became a residential hotel for a number of years. Acquired by new owners in 2000, the hotel has since been renovated and reopened as a luxury hotel. Its lobby still features the original front counter and now includes a wine bar. The Lower Columbia Preservation Society also maintains its offices on the first floor. (Past image, courtesy of CCHS No. 04.183.004.002.)

STAYING THE NIGHT

Hotels such as the Commodore on Fourteenth Street catered to those arriving by ferry at the nearby dock. When the ferry service ended with the opening of the Astoria-Megler Bridge in 1965, these same hotels suffered a steep decline. In response, the Commodore was shuttered and remained closed for 40 years. It sat as a sort of time capsule until new owners restored and reopened it in 2009. (Past image, courtesy of CCHS Ball Studio Collection No. 81.013.301.)

Opening in 1951, the Fur Trader Lounge was located on Fourteenth and Duane Streets in the John Jacob Astor Hotel (originally the Astoria Hotel). Both the hotel and lounge would close in 1965 with the end of the nearby ferry service at the foot of Fourteenth Street. The building reopened as affordable, residential housing in 1984, while the Fur Trader and the building's other storefronts were converted to retail space. (Past image, courtesy of CCHS *Daily Astorian* Collection.)

COMMERCIAL STREET

A longtime Commercial Street mainstay, August Hildebrand's furniture store operated throughout much of the 20th century. Opened in 1905 as Hildebrand & Gore with partner August Gore, it became Hildebrand & Co. by 1910. The store was rebuilt in the same location following the devastating 1922 fire. The new building still bears the Hildebrand name. (Courtesy of CCHS No. 87.058.001.)

The December 8, 1922, fire that destroyed much of downtown Astoria decimated Commercial Street, leaving only two buildings between Eighth and Seventeenth Streets. At Eighth Street, the Spexarth building (seen on the left of both images) survived the flames and, serving as a fire block, helped save other important structures, such as the post office and courthouse. Most buildings east of the Spexarth were built following the fire and many still stand today. (Past image, courtesy of CCHS No. 2044.001.)

The Sherman Transfer Company, seen above, provided moving services out of this location from at least the 1880s through the building's destruction in the 1922 fire. Like many downtown businesses, the Sherman Transfer building was of wooden construction and burned easily. The building's replacement, as with many post-fire structures, was made of reinforced concrete in an effort to prevent future fires. Lucy's Books now occupies this space. (Past image, courtesy of CCHS No. 1218-400S.)

Situated on the northeast corner of Ninth and Commercial Streets, the "M&N" on this building stand for Mary and Nellie Flavel, a mother and daughter from one of Astoria's most prominent Victorian-era families. Though seemingly adhering to many Victorian gender norms, the two women had regular input into the family's business decisions and their own sizable property possessions. (Past image, courtesy of CCHS No. 5713-400Y.)

The Portland company Eastern Outfitters opened their Astoria store a mere three weeks before the 1922 fire. Though a total loss, the company advertised its intention to quickly return. Subsequently, they would occupy a storefront (seen below around 1937) on Commercial Street between Ninth and Tenth Streets for nearly 30 years. Though now empty, restoration efforts are underway to prepare the storefront for new businesses. (Past image, courtesy of CCHS Ball Studio Collection No. 81.013.357.)

Originally built out over a bay and into the Columbia River, much of Astoria's downtown existed atop wood pilings. In the 1910s, a seawall was put in place along the river's edge and the bay under the downtown was partially filled in with sand. Above that, a tile-lined, wooden viaduct was constructed to support the asphalt-paved streets, creating the perfect circumstances for the 1922 fire to spread uncontrollably. (Past image, courtesy of CCHS No. 96.020.036.)

Amid the 1922 fire, the city's downtown streets collapsed, destroying the existing water and electrical systems. These streets had to be reinstalled before the rebuilding above them could begin—though, as the above image illustrates, building construction began while road construction was still underway. A concrete tunnel beneath the streets housed the water and electrical lines, making Astoria among the first cities to submerge its utilities. (Past image, courtesy of CCHS No. 9221-400B.)

I.O.O.F. B'LD'G, 1910 · 4·A.

The International Order of Odd Fellows (IOOF) building was initially constructed in 1882, and served as an important community center. It housed the activities of the IOOF and other fraternal organizations on its upper floors, while the lower level served as retail space. Unfortunately, it was destroyed in the devastating 1922 fire. As seen in the foreground of the image below, only a small portion of the lower level survived. (Both images, courtesy of CCHS No. 80.024.057 [above], 13.046.001.039 [below].)

Following the fire, the IOOF was rebuilt in the same location, again with a lower level dedicated to commercial space and an upper floor for IOOF and other community activities. As membership in the IOOF declined, the building fell into disrepair. In 2018, three local women purchased the building and began its restoration. The following year, they won a national award that sought to honor the often-overlooked role of women in historic preservation. (Past image, courtesy of CCHS No. 08.055.002.)

Though advertising themselves as the "City Book Store," the proprietors of Griffin & Reed, John Griffin and Andrew Reed, offered a variety of items ranging from pianos to sewing machines. They remained on the northeast corner of Tenth and Commercial Streets from the late 1880s through the early 1900s. The site became a bookstore again in 1993 with the opening of Godfather's Books, which is celebrating its 30th anniversary in 2023. (Past image, courtesy of CCHS Sovey Collection No. 52.001.033.)

Prior to the prevalence of telephones, people relied upon telegrams to communicate quickly across great distances. Messages would be received at an office, such as that of the Postal Telegraph Company (pictured above with employees and a delivery truck in 1925), typed out, and delivered to its recipient. Postal Telegraph remained in operation locally until its 1943 merger with Western Union. (Past image, courtesy of CCHS No. 6321-400P.)

August Spexarth sold an eclectic mix of items from this storefront from 1906 through its destruction in the 1922 fire. Merchandise included watches and jewelry, sporting goods, and guns and ammunition. Following the 1922 fire, Spexarth quickly rebuilt this and another property he owned across the street on the south side of Commercial. The "S" atop both buildings marks his last name. A third property on Eighth and Commercial Streets survived the fire. (Past image, courtesy of CCHS Maki Album No. 19.011.004.)

COMMERCIAL STREET

Built following the December 1922 fire, the Associated Building on the northwest corner of Twelfth and Commercial Streets is really three combined buildings: the Hobson, the Copeland, and the Carruthers. Prior to the fire, the Palace Restaurant had operated in this location since the mid-1890s. Like many downtown businesses, it moved to a temporary location after the fire, reopening on Commercial and Twentieth Streets. (Past image, courtesy of CCHS Maki Album No. 19.011.004.)

Throughout the 1910s, the Crystal Theater presented feature films alongside Vaudeville acts. Unique among the city's theaters, the Crystal often booked Black performers as part of its regular rotation. An early troupe, Billy and Leonce Johnsons, earned high praise in the local paper, noting, "it will be a real treat to see them." Tickets sold 10¢ for adults and 5¢ for children with the proceeds benefitting the local high school. (Past image, courtesy of CCHS Maki Album No. 19.011.004.)

Located on the southeast corner of Twelfth and Commercial Streets, the Liberty Theatre is one of Astoria's most iconic establishments. Built following the 1922 fire, the theater served as a movie house for a number of years and was featured in the movie *The Black Stallion* (1979). Restored and renovated in the early 2000s, the Liberty Theater now showcases a variety of performances including music, dance, and film. (Past image, courtesy of CCHS Reuben Jensen Collection No. 98.036.002.)

Looking east on Commercial from Twelfth Street reveals a row of structures built following the 1922 fire, beginning with the Astoria Building featuring the Liberty Theatre and ending at the Astoria Hotel. The buildings have remained relatively unchanged, but other important alterations have occurred, including to traffic flow. In the above photograph from the late 1940s, cars are traveling both directions, while in the image below they are only moving west to east. (Past image, courtesy of CCHS No. 4368-400A.)

Opening on Commercial Street in 1898, Utzinger and Sons specialized in cigar manufacturing. It expanded its offerings to include newspapers by 1906, becoming Utzinger's News Depot. A decade later, the family business became Utzinger's Book Store. It remained in this original location between Twelfth and Fourteenth Streets until the building's destruction in the 1922 fire. As Uzinger's Book Store, it operated out of several successive storefronts along Commercial Street into the mid-1980s. (Past image, courtesy of CCHS No. 1907-400U.)

The walkway to the left of the building marks where Thirteenth Street would be. Astoria was originally laid out by two separate developers who, in competition with one another, failed to make their plans align. Consequently, the city blocks to the west of what would be Thirteenth are slightly larger than those to the east, creating odd bends in the city streets. Thirteenth Street in Astoria only exists for a single block between Duane and Exchange Streets. (Past image, courtesy of CCHS No. 6738-400G.)

Looking west from Fourteenth Street, much changed before and after the 1922 fire. On this end of Commercial Street only the Young Building—seen in the right of the lower image—survived the blaze, though its interior was gutted. Originally constructed in 1916, post-fire, the first floor was pushed back and metal poles were installed to support the second level. This was done to widen Commercial Street in order to accommodate increased auto traffic. (Past image, courtesy of CCHS No. 01.036.007.)

Businessman Wah Sing—pictured above at center with his sons Quong Chan, left, and Tong Chan, right, around 1913—operated his Merchant Tailor Shop on Commercial between Fourteenth and Fifteenth Streets from approximately 1902 through the 1922 fire. Following the fire, Greenburg's furniture became a longtime occupant of the space, with this and the building immediately east eventually being combined to appear as a single structure. (Past image, courtesy of CCHS No. 00.021.006.)

Firefighters from four different Astoria companies prepare to compete in a Firemen's muster (tournament) around 1890. Musters allowed firefighters to display their skills and earn money for equipment. Their popularity led to the formation of women's and junior teams. Standing at 15th and Commercial Streets, the undeveloped area behind the competitors holds Tidal Rock, which early sailors used to judge safe landing in Astoria. This site is now a community park. (Past image, courtesy of CCHS No. 4720-565.)

When Astoria celebrated the city's centennial in 1911, local business owner Victor Rodas joined in the celebratory spirit, advertising to the thousands of visitors drawn by the centennial events. The part of Commercial Street at Sixteenth Street where Rodas had his small market no longer exists, replaced by a roadway interchange. Immediately north of this location, Astoria's Nordic Heritage Park was dedicated in June 2022 and celebrates Astoria's various Nordic communities. (Past image, courtesy of CCHS No. 22.001.069.)

CHAPTER

AROUND TOWN

Looking south from the corner of Eighth and Bond Streets (now Marine Drive), several important Astoria structures are visible. Moving up the street on the right are the post office, the courthouse, the Flavel mansion, and McClure School. On the left, the Spexarth building sits one block up, marking the edge of the 1922 fire. (Courtesy of CCHS No. 29018-900.)

LENGTH 2.19 FT 5 3/4 IN

960 FLAG POLE FOR ASTORIA ORE CENTENNIAL PARK LONGEST FLAG POLE IN THE WORLD

Plans for the 1911 celebration of Astoria's centennial involved raising a giant flagpole at the highest point at Centennial (now Shively) Park. Midway through being raised the flagpole broke, crashing back to the ground. Though the flagpole was abandoned, the celebration went forward and included a number of parades, band performances, a historical pageant, and fireworks displays. Two picnic shelters that would have flanked the giant flagpole remain in Shively Park. (Past image, courtesy of CCHS No. 1507-111.)

In the late 1940s, local groups organized to preserve the history of the 1811 Astoria fort. They created a park on the original site, complete with a reconstructed fort and interpretive sign. Initially, this sign celebrated only a small portion of those involved in the city's founding, ignoring the significant contributions of local Native Americans, Hawaiians, and African Americans. The sign was updated in 2022 to better reflect this broader story. (Past image, courtesy of CCHS No. 13.040.010.)

As a city built upon steep hills, Astoria has several walking paths in places where car travel proves impractical. Often, these include some sort of assistance to the would-be walker—whether handrails or low steps. Among the more unique of these, the so-called "pigeon steps" on Eleventh Street consist of small horizontal ridges that help prevent walkers from slipping and reward hikers at the top with a tremendous view. (Past image, courtesy of CCHS No. 7437-900.)

Immortalized in the opening sequences of the 2005 movie *The Ring Two*, the small park seen from the corner of Seventh and Franklin Streets once housed McClure School. Built in 1883, the school taught all grades through 1910 and continued as an elementary school until 1917. Taking its name from the earlier school, friends of McClure Park used the steep hill on the south side of the block to install a giant slide. (Past image, courtesy of CCHS No. 1314.002.)

Lovell Auto Company owner Sherman Lovell fought back against calls to dynamite his recently constructed showroom on Fourteenth between Duane and Exchange Streets during the 1922 fire. The building survived the fire and would provide a home to many displaced businesses. The Blue Mouse Theatre was among the first to establish itself in the repurposed structure, creating a theater on the upper level just three weeks after the fire. (Past image, courtesy of CCHS No. 1466-400L.)

The Riviera Theatre on Eleventh and Bond (now Marine Drive) Streets first opened in June 1925, providing an additional space locally for silent and vaudeville acts. It would close at the end of the 1926 season and not reopen until 1933. Continuing as the Riviera Theatre for the next 26 years, it closed again in 1959. Currently operated as the Columbian Theatre, it continues to show both studio and independent films. (Past image, courtesy of CCHS Ball Studio Collection No. 81.013.355.)

Survivors from the 1846 wreck of the USS *Shark* inscribed the event on the so-called "Shark Rock." In the early 20th century, the rock was placed in the middle of Niagara Street. Since moved to a museum, the area is now marked by the longtime community grocery the Peter Pan Market—appearing below in its original location and above, having taken over the storefront immediately to the west, where it moved in the late 1930s. (Past image, courtesy of CCHS No. 18.069.001.)

AROUND TOWN

Sven Gimre first opened a shoemaking and repair shop on Bond Street in 1892 and started selling factory-made shoes from this location in the following decade. Following the 1922 fire, Sven moved his shop to Fourteenth between Bond and Commercial Streets. Celebrating a century in this same location in 2023, and operated by Sven's descendants, Gimre's is the oldest family-run shoe store in Oregon. (Past image, courtesy of CCHS Ball Studio Collection No. 81.013.590.)

Constructed in 1916, the Young Men's Christian Association (YMCA) building survived the 1922 fire when children who belonged to the YMCA used water from its swimming pool to douse the encroaching flames. The YMCA remained in operation in Astoria through the mid-1980s but closed due to financial hardship. The building has since been restored and now hosts several small businesses. (Past image, courtesy of CCHS No. 96.047.001.)

Occupying a more modest space, the Young Women's Christian Association (YWCA) building sat immediately across the street from that of the YMCA. It was built into an existing home turned boardinghouse following the destruction of the original Astoria YWCA in the 1922 fire. Closing in the mid-1980s alongside the YMCA, the building sat empty for a time but was eventually reopened as a popular daycare center. (Past image, courtesy of CCHS *Daily Astorian* Collection.)

The Astoria Savings Bank was rebuilt in 1923 on its original, pre-1922 fire, foundation, incorporating the vault from the earlier building into the new structure. Like many banks around the country, it closed in 1929 and never reopened. In 1939, city hall was moved to this location to be closer to the center of Astoria's downtown. (Past image, courtesy of CCHS No. 120-400A.)

Constructed in 1904 as Astoria's city hall, this building on Sixteenth Street between Duane and Exchange Streets, initially housed the city's police station, courtroom, and public library. With the city hall moving to a new location in 1939, the building would become, in turn, a USO, the original Maritime Museum, and finally Clatsop County Historical Society's Heritage Museum. This museum features multiple exhibits exploring the history of Astoria and Clatsop County. (Past image, courtesy of CCHS No. 7790-966.)

MEMORIAL TO SOLDIERS OF WORLD WAR. ASTORIA ORE

After World War I, communities throughout the United States erected monuments to the so-called "doughboy"—a popular term for the often-young members of the US Infantry. As with many such monuments, Astoria's memorial in the Uniontown neighborhood features a mass-produced doughboy sculpture, a bronze by John Paulding entitled *Over the Top at Cantigny*, model 2043-C. The only other known copy of this particular model is in Catskills, New York. (Past image, courtesy of CCHS No. 6777-908.)

AROUND TOWN

The 125-foot-high Astoria Column was dedicated on July 22, 1926, as part of the three-day Astoria Founder's Celebration—that also included the dedication of the Doughboy monument—and the Columbia River Historical Expedition. As part of an effort to revive the railroad industry, this expedition, hosted by the Great Northern Railroad, sent travelers on a 12-day voyage out of Chicago to visit important historical sites throughout the northwestern United States. (Past image, courtesy of CCHS No. 3343-738.)

Originally constructed for beer production as the North Pacific Brewery, the building that became the Uppertown Firefighters Museum was shuttered with the local passage of Prohibition, the outlawing of alcohol, in 1915. In 1928, the building was redesigned to serve as the Uppertown Fire Station and continued in this capacity until 1960. In 1990, it was reopened as the Uppertown Firefighters Museum featuring historic firefighting engines and equipment. (Past image, courtesy of CCHS No. 3343-738.)

AROUND TOWN

A working jail from 1914 through 1976, the one-time Clatsop County Jail now houses the Oregon Film Museum, which celebrates Oregon's long filmmaking tradition. Beginning with the first feature film made in Oregon—*The Fisherman's Bride,* shot in Astoria in 1909—more than 300 movies and television shows have been created in the state. The jail itself has served as the backdrop for at least three Oregon films, most notably 1985's cult classic *The Goonies.* (Past image, courtesy of CCHS No. 10.030.001.)

Overlooking Youngs Bay on Astoria's South Slope, Tapiola Park once featured an outdoor, heated swimming pool. Closed in the late-1990s with the construction of the new, indoor Astoria Aquatic Center, the Astoria Skate Park has since been built in its place. Named for a Finnish forest god, Tapiola Park currently includes several sports fields and a playground built to resemble many of Astoria's historic structures. (Past image, courtesy of CCHS No. 97.013.003.9.)

AROUND TOWN

LONG-TERM
RESIDENTS

Peter and Maria Larson constructed their home in the Uppertown neighborhood around 1880. Following Peter's untimely death in 1893, Maria began renting rooms in the house to boarders. The Larsons continued to live at this location into the 1950s, with daughter Ester, a local school teacher, being the last to call the place home. (Courtesy of CCHS No. 4548-960.)

In 1858, Alfred Crosby's home was built on what would become Sixth and Commercial Streets (seen below in 1860). Demolished in 1929, a service station and then a small park and playground followed. The dragon mural (seen above) was painted by Astoria High School students in 2019 and honors the longtime business in the building back of the park. Lum Quing Grocery operated in this location from the early 1920s through 1964. (Past image, courtesy of CCHS No. 482-960.)

Built for Swedish immigrant and businessman Benjamin Young in 1888, this large home in Uppertown now serves as a bed and breakfast. Young (pictured above, middle row, left) poses around 1900 with his wife, Christina (middle row, right), and their children. Daughter Clara (seated back row, center) graduated from medical school in 1907. She was a respected doctor in Astoria, serving as the county health officer and teaching at the local nursing school. (Past image, courtesy of CCHS No. 4377-00Y.)

Located in Astoria's Uniontown neighborhood at the west end of town, these two historic homes date to the late 1800s. Originally a Finnish immigrant community, many Uniontown residents worked in the fishing industry, with their homes built on the hill above the fish canneries that dotted the river below. The name Uniontown derives from one of these early canneries. (Past image, courtesy of CCHS No. 4230-960.)

LONG-TERM RESIDENTS

Uppertown on the east end of Astoria contains a mix of 19th- and early-20th-century working-class homes alongside those constructed in the mid to late-20th century and a handful of Victorian-era mansions. This home, on Thirty-Fourth and Irvine Streets, exemplifies the first type. Beginning in the early 1900s, it has been the residence of a carpenter, a bricklayer, a painter, and several fishermen. (Past image, courtesy of CCHS No. 7852-960.)

Longtime Astoria architect John Wicks designed and built this home for himself and his family in 1919. Wicks designed many residential and commercial properties and was instrumental in the reconstruction of the city's downtown following the devastating 1922 fire. His daughter Ebba followed in his footsteps, becoming a renowned architect in her own right. Many of Astoria's mid-century structures are of Ebba's design, including the Astoria Public Library. (Past image, courtesy of CCHS No. 6553-960.)

LONG-TERM RESIDENTS

Publisher of the *Morning Astorian* newspaper of nearly 30 years, John Dellinger, alongside his wife, Gertrude, had this house on Sixteenth Street built in 1919. Dellinger had a long journalism career, establishing numerous papers on his way west from Pennsylvania. In the early 1910s, he would take up cranberry farming as a backup career. Gertrude continued in the cranberry business following her husband's death. (Past image, courtesy of CCHS No. 11.049.004.)

Above, Francis Thomas, queen of the 1903 Astoria Regatta, returns to her home via horse-drawn carriage after a day of reigning over the city's annual celebration. The house, on Fourteenth and Grand Streets, would undergo multiple remodels and, becoming the Elmore Apartments by 1931, a dramatic change in its use. Named for cannery owners Samuel and Mary Elmore, the couple lived here from approximately 1905 through their deaths in 1910 and 1921, respectively. (Past image, courtesy of CCHS No. 435-100.)

LONG-TERM RESIDENTS

Schoolteacher Helen Dickinson moved into this home on Franklin Street with her parents in the 1880s and, following their deaths, continued to live there into the 1920s. During her career, Helen taught elementary students in at least three of the local public schools: McClure above Astoria's downtown, Adair in Uppertown (now the site of Astor Elementary), and Shively on Sixteenth and Exchange Streets near Helen's home. (Past image, courtesy of CCHS No. 13.040.015.)

As seen below, in the 1890s Thaddeus and Georgia Trullinger lived in the home on the left, while Wellington and Jennie Howell occupied the one on the right. Both homes would meet different fates. The Wellington house was torn down in the 1930s, becoming a parking lot for the Trullinger home next door. In 1986, this house was converted to the popular community radio station KMUN-FM, and is still used for broadcasting today. (Past image, courtesy of CCHS No. 11,637.)

LONG-TERM RESIDENTS

By 1890, Herman and Henrietta Prael had established themselves in the above home on the corner of Ninth and Grand Streets. Herman kept himself busy working as a bookkeeper for the Clatsop Mill, president of his own company, Prael-Eigner Transfer Co., and as city treasurer. Following Herman's death in the early 1930s, Henrietta remained in their home for a few more years before moving elsewhere. The house was demolished soon after. (Past image, courtesy of CCHS No. 1027-960.)

Mary Flavel's sisters Sophia and Eliza Boelling stand on the porch of the home on the southwest corner of Eighth and Exchange Streets. Originally built by their parents, Conrad and Philipina Boelling, Sophia and Eliza remained in this home until their deaths in 1940 and 1941, respectively. The house has been moved and now sits immediately west of its original location. (Past image, courtesy of CCHS No. 12.001.040)

Built as a retirement home for Capt. George Flavel, he, his wife Mary, and their adult daughters Nellie and Katie moved into this house in 1886. The Clatsop County Historical Society assumed care of the home in the 1950s, using it as a history museum. Opening the Heritage Museum in the mid-1980s, the historical society then converted this historic home into the Flavel House Museum and restored it to its Victorian-era grandeur. (Past image, courtesy of CCHS Flavel Collection No. 02.004.088.)

DISCOVER THOUSANDS OF LOCAL HISTORY BOOKS FEATURING MILLIONS OF VINTAGE IMAGES

Arcadia Publishing, the leading local history publisher in the United States, is committed to making history accessible and meaningful through publishing books that celebrate and preserve the heritage of America's people and places.

Find more books like this at
www.arcadiapublishing.com

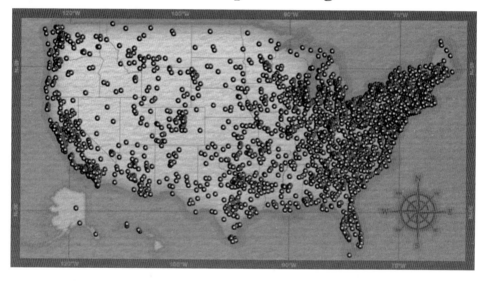

Search for your hometown history, your old stomping grounds, and even your favorite sports team.